YOU KEEP
ON GOING
THE OTHER
WAY

YOU KEEP
ON GOING
THE OTHER
WAY

BREN DANIELS

YOU KEEP ON GOING THE OTHER WAY

Scripture quotations marked KJV are from the Holy Bible, King James Version (Authorized Version). First published in 1611. Quoted from the KJV Classic Reference Bible, Copyright © 1983 by The Zondervan Corporation.

iUniverse books may be ordered through booksellers or by contacting:

iUniverse
1663 Liberty Drive
Bloomington, IN 47403
www.iuniverse.com
1-800-Authors (1-800-288-4677)

ISBN: 978-1-5320-8570-3 (sc)
ISBN: 978-1-5320-8571-0 (hc)
ISBN: 978-1-5320-8569-7 (e)

Library of Congress Control Number: 2019916237

Print information available on the last page.

iUniverse rev. date: 10/14/2019

DO IT
GOD
WAY

Introduction

This Book is an Inspirational Book to encourage you to stay on the right path. And to choose the right way to go.

Matthew 7:13 Enter ye in at the strait gate: for wide is the gate, and broad is the way, that leadeth to destruction, and many there be which go in there at:

Matthew 7:14 Because strait is the gate, and narrow is the way, which leadeth unto life, and few there be that find it. This Book is also about choices that we make in life. We can choose Jesus Christ as our LORD and savior for he is the right way. Are we can do our own thing. Which have severe consequences. If you let Jesus guide your life and make him as your LORD and savior you will have a successful life even eternal life. For there is life after death. The malefactor which was also on the cross said to Jesus. LORD remember me when thou comest into thy kingdom. And Jesus said unto him, Verily I say unto thee, Today shalt thou be with me in paradise. Luke23:43

Contents

Coming To Church

Destination

Don't Give UP

Favour

Judging

Love

Need

Praise

Pray

Right Way

Salvation

Staying With God

Test

Victory

Wrong Way

1

You Come To Church All The Time

Some people come to church year after year, Sunday after Sunday, Wednesday after Wednesday, Friday after Friday. And still in the same shape they have been in. Never change. I am God I can fix it if you let me. You don't have to stay in the shape you are in. You don't have to keep acting like you got it, and know you don't. Some things you should be done mastered. Some things you go thru you should know how to deal with. Year after year month after month. You still haven't changed. You need to make up your mind. You are going to sell out to me. Then and then only, the times you come to church. You will get something out of me.

2

You Need To Halt In Church

———❈———

I see what you do. You come to church, you talk about people. You pray in tongues and after church you treat people wrong. You need to halt in church. You pray in tongues, jerk like you feel something. You call my name. Then when church is over. You speak to people, but it's not real. You smile at people and it's fake. You get home from church. You talk about what someone done or what they had on. Instead of talking about my word. And what you heard them speak about my word. You need to just halt in church and get it right.

You Keep Coming To The Altar Without Change

It's good to come to the altar and get it right. But somethings you should have mastered by now. Year after year, month after month. You keep coming to the altar for the same reason. I give out too much power, for you not to get it right. The problem is not me. The problem is you. You need to realize what your doing. You see the most time you spend is out church. Your only in church a few hours. So, your altar should be carried every where you go. And if the Holy Ghost convict you for something you have done. You can immediately repent. Instead of waiting unto you get back to church. What if you don't make it back to church. When you come to the altar, there should be a change. How is it that you go back the same. Because you are not allowing me to change you. So when you do come to the altar allow me to change you. So when you go sit down your label want be in vain. And there will be a change.

Quit Faking It When You Come To Church

You come to church smile at people, knowing you don't like them. You get in church even sing in the choir. Knowing you don't mean it. You even pray for people laying on hands. Really don't mean it. You keep faking what you're doing. When all you got to do is confess to me. Lord, I don't like them, Lord I don't like to sing in the choir. Are whatever position you hold. Are Lord I got a problem praying for them. If you will confess to me. What you feel, then I can deliver you. You don't have to pretend. Knowing deep down you are a fake within. You may have people to think you are real, but not me. For I know what you feel that's why I am saying this. So you can get it right and I can set you free.

It's Time For People In Church To Get It Right

This poem is for some and not for all. Get it right and get it now. As long as you have been in church you should know how. Some of you have been saved for years. You suppose to be teaching the younger ones how to be saved. Through my word. But I don't see that. You will put your mouth on them, instead of praying for them. Remember you wasn't always like you are. As long as you have been saved. You should have mastered some things. You should know how to comfort people, love people, be real with people, have compassion on people, and be merciful to people. You should have mastered these, but yet you're not able too. For you have need one that could teach you. For you haven't learned yet. Learn me and learn my ways. Because it's time for the Church to get it right. Why it is still day.

What Will Be At The End Of Your Life

What will be waiting on you after you leave this life. You are either one step from Heaven or one step from Hell. When you leave this world you will step into eternity. And eternity is for a long time. Make sure when you leave this world God knows you. It's not if you say you know God. But it's if God knows you.

Don't Wait Until It's Too Late

In this life some people may be saying. I will wait until I am leaving this world to get saved. What if you don't get a chance to say you want to be save. Just like myself I stay stored up in prayer. Because sometimes things may happen so quick you may not be able to ask God to help you. But if you have already stored up in prayer. God will remember your prayers. That's why the Bible says pray without ceasing. I Thess. 5:17

8

Where Will You End Up

If you serve God heaven will be your home. I am living a saved life because I want to see Jesus. And I want to be in his presence. Threw out all eternity. I choose Jesus for the rest of my life. I will end up wherever Jesus wants me to be. And no one can't stop me. If I continue to abide in the word of God. God will bless me to end up were I need to be.

9

Keep Moving

No matter what's going on around you. Keep moving. Jesus was always moving. If people don't receive you. Go somewhere else. Where they will receive you. Even Jesus says if they don't receive you. If you enter into a place and they don't receive you shake the dust off your feet. Matt 10:14 And whosoever shall not receive you, nor hear your words, when ye depart out of that house or city, shake the dust off your feet.

10

There Is Purpose On Your Life

There is purpose on your life. You were born for a reason. And you was born for God purpose. But if you don't surrender to God. How can he show you the plan he has for your life. You were born for greatness. Greatness is upon you. Purpose is on you. So will you give your life to God. So he can show you the purpose he has for your life.

11

Jesus Has A Good Plan For Your Life

❦

Jesus has a awesome plan for your life. It's not until you give him your life. He can show you what he wants you to do. If you acknowledge him in all your ways. He will direct your path. If you let God work the plan he has for your life. You will have a good life. God has planned only good things for your life. For he says I know the plans I have for your life. And It's to give you an expected end.

12

Jesus Loves You

———❊———

Jesus loves you so much. That's why he came to this earth to redeem mankind back to God. Jesus can fix anything that troubles you. But you have to cast all your cares upon him because he cares for you. So whatever you are going through. Remember Jesus loves and cares for you.

Don't Give Up

Don't give up and don't throw in the towel. Troubles don't last always. It don't always rain the sun will come out again. Weeping may endure for a night but joy cometh in the morning. You will smile again. You will live again. And if you trust God. The joy of the LORD will be your strength.

Change Will Come When You Trust God

You may be going through but change will come. Hold your head up and keep the faith. There is a time and a season for everything under the sun. God has a way to turn your bad days into good days. Just like when a woman is pregnant she may be going through those 9 months and all kind of sickness. But when the baby come what joy she has. So she forgets the pain. And when God turn it around. You will forget all the trouble you went through. For your change will come.

Your Better Days Are Ahead

Better days are ahead for you. Everything you go through God is making you. If God brought you to it. He will bring you through it.

God is in charge of everything that happens. He can turn things around suddenly.

Your better days will come suddenly.
Suddenly you will be happy.
Suddenly you will get the joy you want.
Suddenly you will get the house you want.
Suddenly you will get the car you want.
Suddenly everything will change.

16

God Can Give You Favour

———— ❊ ————

God can give you favour with him and also with man. It's God who holds all things in his hands. You don't have to seek favour from people. Seek favour from God. And God can move on man's heart to bless you with favour. Put God first and man second. For its God who holds all things in his hands. Jobs, Houses, Cars, Finances, Businesses, whatever you need to succeed. God got just what you need. So seek the favour of God and not of man. To God belong all things and not man.

Don't Find Fault In Another

People always looking for fault in another. As if they do nothing wrong. They always get in church and say. People this and people that. Why don't you just pray for people. You put out more energy in saying what they do. Instead of praying for them, Don't look for fault in another. Pray for them, if you know they are in trouble. Don't say people this or people that. Meaning they do it this way or that way. Don't look for fault just pray, pray, pray. And quit looking for fault in your brother.

18

Treating People Right

In this world many things you will go through. But you just make sure you treat people right. You cannot dictate how people treat you. But you can control how you treat them. So be careful that you treat people right. Because Galatians 6:7 Be not deceived; God is not mocked; for whatsoever a man soweth, that shall he also reap. It may take years down the road before a person reap. So if you plant squash. When harvest time come. Do not expect watermelon. Because you didn't plant that. Whatever you plant that is what you will receive in your due season.

19

Treating People Wrong

The word of God says. And as ye would that men should do to you, do ye also to them likewise. Luke 6:31. So don't treat people wrong. For you don't want anyone treating you wrong. For what you do to someone will surely come back to you. It could be later on in life. You will surely reap what you sow. And you will remember who you wronged. And they will remember also if they wronged you. The Bible says God brings all things back to your remembrance.

Quit Treating Your Brother Wrong

How can you treat your neighbor, brother, sister, mother, aunt, uncle, cousin, and family are even friends wrong. But, still say you are saved. You should set an example for them. Even though they may not care for you. Are want to come around you. Don't do them wrong, even if they disagree with what you believe in. For God loves charity and this he love above all. That you say and that you do. Charity is above all and that is true. So don't treat your brother wrong, treat them right. For this pleasing in God sight.

Quit Preaching On People, Saying Your Own Words

Some people, not all get up in church. Speak on people instead of saying my word. If my word don't draw them neither can yours. I allow test, triles and tribulation too. Things come their way to warn them. To make them change. Yet, still after they have been delivered from whatever sickness, disease, colds, flu, and other symptoms too. They go back to doing the same things, they were doing before they were sick. So quit speaking on them and tell them my word. If my word don't change them neither can your word.

Don't Put Your Mouth On God Anointy

Be careful who you put your mouth on. You don't understand them. You don't like them, your jealous of them. Your even envies of them, but don't voice your opinion about them, God says touch not my anointed, do my prophets no harm. So be careful who you put your mouth on.

23

People May Look At You Funny

People may look at you funny when you shout. They may even say it's not real. But, always remember God knows your heart for he is near. Let them look at you funny. When you shout, when clap your hand, when you pray in tongues and even when you pray. But, just remember who helps you along the way. The Lord our righteousness. He's the one who helps us. So don't worry about what people say, or how they look at you. When you are giving God the glory. For when they were in the club, at a football game or basketball game, etc. they weren't worrying if anyone was looking at them funny.

Be Careful How You Treat People
It Will Come Up Again

People may be doing you wrong. When people do you bad. It will come up again. The Bible says the battle do not belong to you it belongs to the LORD. You just make sure you are right. And go ahead on. When you have done right by people. You can look for someone to do right by you. For whatever you do unto men. The same will be done unto you. If you are looking for good to come to you. Then do good by others.

25

How Can You Not Love Me

You read my word, I tell you just how I am. I don't lie. I can't lie. I am God, I created the stars at night. I calmed the winds and said peace be still. I got power over life and death. I got power over all things, because I made all things. You have needs I can supply them. You have wants, I can give you your heart's desire. You want love, I am a God of love. You want peace, I can give that to you. So, how can you not love me. Think about it and know I'm the one you need to be loving.

26

Show Love To All People

If you see someone know matter, what they look like, how they smell. Let them know Jesus loves them and he cares. Show love to all people near and far. Let them know God loves and cares for them also. We that are saved should show the world we care. Not acting more Holy than thou. But letting others know thru our testimonies. It's by the grace of God we are where we are for we weren't always saved. And because of the love of God we are saved. And that's why we should show love to all men where ever we are and to let people know we love them know matter who they are.

God Loves You Unconditionally

God loves you unconditionally. It doesn't matter where you come from. You may be in a family that doesn't have much. But God is the one who blesses men to get wealth. So, he can bless you with wealth. Well, God blessed you to have the wealth you have. You see whatever shape you are in. God still loves you. And he loves you unconditionally. And that's God. For God is love.

28

Show Love To Your Neighbor

———— ❋ ————

We have to show love to everyone. It does not matter their color or who they are. You have to love people the way Jesus did. The Bible says for God so loved the world that he gave his only begotten son. That whosoever believeth in him shall not perish but have everlasting life. So God wants us to love the way he loves.

God Is Everything You Need

You need a healer, God is. You need a helper, God is. You need a provider, God is. You need a deliver, God is. You need a way maker, God is. You need a lawyer, God is. You need love, God is. You need comfort, God is. You need someone you can depend on, God is. You need someone who will never do you wrong. God is someone who will never leave you or forsake you. God is everything you need. Make him your Savior and you will be able to say. God is all these things and much much more. Because you will learn thru triles and test. God is all you need and he's the best.

30

God Can Give You What You Need

God can give you what you need. He said you have not because you ask not. He said to ask and it shall be given. He says seek and you shall find. Knock and the door shall be open. When you come to God you got to believe he is a rewarder of them that diligently seek him. God got everything you need.

Be Careful Who You Connect With

You have to be careful who you connect with. The Bible says Be not deceived evil communication corrupt good manners I Cor. 15:33. You have to be careful who you tell your vision and dreams with everyone may not want your success. You may need to ask God who you need to connect with. Because he knows who will always be there for you and who want let you down.

Don't Let Nothing Hinder Your Walk With God

Don't let nothing hinder your walk with God. First of all don't see nothing bigger than God in your life. God is in charge of everything. There's nothing you go through God does not already know about. He says there nothing new under the sun. Ecc. 1:9 The thing that hath been, is that which shall be; and that which is done is that which shall be done; and there is no new thing under the sun.

Praise The Lord

It's a good thing to give praise unto the Lord. It's good to praise him in the dance. You can dance for Jesus. You may use to dance for the devil. If you did, you shouldn't be ashamed to dance for Jesus. So when you go to church, praise him in the dance and clap your hands. You see when you know God has been good to you and you appreciate. What God has done for you. Know one want have to tell you to praise him. You will praise the Lord for his goodness. So praise him all ye people. Praise the Lord.

Sing Unto The Lord

Sing unto the Lord a new song. Make melody in your heart to God. Just think on how good, God has been to you. And that's something to sing about. Sing how he deliver you, healed you, set you free, been there for you in times of need. Sing when you're driving your car, sing when you're at home, sing on your job, make melody in your heart unto the Lord. Sing because he has been good, sing because he has been kind. Sing unto the Lord. Sing, Sing, Sing.

Put On The Whole Armour

Put on the whole armour that you may be able to withstand against the wiles of the devil. You cannot win over the devil without the power of God. For God says Behold I have given you power to tread over serpents and scorpions, and over all the powers of the enemy and nothing shall not by any means hurt you. God has equip you with power.

36

Take Your Joy Back

The Bible says the kingdom of heaven suffeth violence but the violence taketh it by force. You need joy take it back. You need strength take it back. You got to take what you need through prayer. God will back you up when you believe he can. Faith moves God. Take your joy back.

You Need To Pray

Now you are living in perilous times. Things are not like they use to be. Things you use to get by with. Things you use to do, is about to start judging you. You feel you can just go to Church for just a form or fashion. Are just to let people say. I was there at church. So, you feel they want talk about you. Saying she has back slide. But remember, I am the important one. You need to just quit faking it. And remember you are living in last days. And remember, it's going to take prayer to make it. So you need to just pray, pray, pray, and quit faking it.

38

Pray, Pray, Pray

❖

You want to stay saved. Pray. You want to stay victorious in Christ Jesus. Pray. You want yokes to be broken off your life. Pray. You want to defeat your enemies. Pray. You want a successful future. Pray. The only way to be what God, want you to be and to have a victorious future. You have to pray, pray, pray. So let's pray.

You Got To Be A Prayer Warrior

You got to be a prayer warrior. Praying all the time praying anywhere. Know that God hears you when you pray. You got to pray when everything seems to be okay. You got to pray when things are not okay. When you pray God listens. He hears everything that you say. He says you will have whatsoever you say. So what are you saying. Keep on praying.

40

Take Your Peace Back

The devil comes to rob, steal, kill and destroy. You need peace. God can give you peace. All you have to do is stay prayerful. Prayer changes every situation. If you would just pray your peace will remain. Because if you cast all your cares on God. Your peace will remain. Because you will know God will take care of it.

What Way Are You Going

Are you going down the right path.

Are you frustrated.

Are you confuse.

Are you afraid of the unknown. Well if you give Jesus Christ your life. You will not be afraid. For to be absent in the body is to be present with the LORD. And for me to live is Christ and to die is to gain.

42

People May Do You Evil, But Still Do Them Good

People may do you evil, but still do them good people may have mistreat you. But still treat them nice. Because you will give an account for how you treat people. Not how they treat you. They will have to give in account to God for how they treat you. The battle is not yours it belongs to the LORD. It's just nice to be nice. So be nice.

43

Watch How You Treat People

You better be careful how you treat God's people. You need to be gentle with God people. For God says touch not my anointy and do my prophets no harm. God means what he say. He says it was better for him that a millstone were hanged about his neck, and he cast into the sea, than that he should offend one of these little ones. God means exactly what he says.

Which Way Will You Chose

The choice is yours. Who will you serve? God doesn't force anyone to serve him. The choice you makes determine where your eternity will be spent. Choose God and Heaven is your home. Choose the devil and hell will be your eternity. So choose the way of the Lord. And heaven will be a sure foundation. It will be your home.

God Is Looking And He Is Booking

What will your book say at the end of your life. Because only what you do for Christ will last.

Will God be able to say you served him faithfully.

Will God be able to say you helped in the Church.

Will God be able to say you showed love to everyone etc.

What will your book say about you. Remember God is looking and he is booking.

46

Doing Right Will Pay Off

Nothing given to God is wasted. When you do right. It will come back to you. God is faithful that promises. God will reward you for doing right. You just keep pleasing God. And one day he will say well done thy good and faithful servant. God rewards for doing right.

47

Now Look To The Right

Have you been saved for even a year. Are even a day. If you are letting Jesus be your light. You will shine brighter every day and every night. As long as you look to the right. And continue to let Jesus guide your life. Your future will be successful. And you will do good all the days of your life. As long as you let Jesus guide your life.

If You Are On The Right Track, Stay On It. And Keep Following God

Keep following God if you are on the right track. Don't look to the left and you want turn back. As long as you keep your eyes on God you will turn out alright. Following God you can never go wrong. For he will help you to overcome. So keep on the right track. And you will never want to turn back.

49

God Is Keeping Record

God is keeping record. What will you do to show God you really want to serve him. For God sees and he also knows. And whatever you do. It's being recorded and one day. Your book will be open. And only what you do for Christ will last.

50

It's Coming Up Again

In this life don't think that you do people wring and that's the end of it. God told me one time. He is looking and he is booking. God keeps record of everything you do. Whether it's good or bad. You might get by. But you don't get away. God will give everyman according to what he or she has done.

51

Choose To Live Right On Earth

The way you live your life it's up to you. You have free will to choose God or not. He does not force you to serve him. He says in Joshua 24:15 And if it seem evil unto you to serve the LORD, choose you this day whom ye will serve; God gives you the choice. He lets you make the decision to serve him or not. He do not force himself on you. It's up to you to choose to live right on this earth. Because of the choices you make will determine where you will spend eternity.

You Going Around Saying Your Saved But, You Still Act Like The Devil

You go around saying your saved but you still act like the devil. You talk about people, you lie, you curse, you drink, you smoke, you gossip, you complain, you murmur. You do all I say don't do. In my word, I say speak evil of know man, you still do. I also say all liars shall have their part in the lake of fire, you still do. You curse, I say everyone shall give account for every idle word. You drink I say you shouldn't drink strong drink. You complain, I hate when you complain and murmur. You smoke and it suppose too be my temple. You do all the things my word is against. But, yet you claim to be saved. Quit deceiving yourself. For know unclean thing shall enter into heaven. Get it right, and get it now. For you shall be judged with the unrighteous. Because everyone will be judged according to the things which he or she has done.

Being Saved Is More Than Saying It

People say I'm saved. I've been in this thing a long time. Well, being saved is not just words. It's living something. Some people want a form of godliness but denying the truth, God word say. People want to say I wear long dresses. I don't wear make-up. I don't wear nail polish, etc. But it's not so much in what you wear. But, that is important too, but, it's how you live. You can wear long dresses, no make-up, no nail polish, and stay home and don't go know were. But still be on your way to hell. It's not in what you say. It's how you live will show if you are saved.

Everyday Should Be A Saved Day When Your Saved

Don't think being saved is on Sunday, are church, Wednesday at bible study, or even Friday at prayer. Being saved should be 365 days in a year. Being saved should be a life style. Its God name that your representing. So you should want to be Holy every day. And walk right, talk right, and do what's right. For being saved should be done and lived 365 days in a year. And that's being saved.

It's An Honor To Serve The Lord

Why would you want to do it any other way. Except God way. It's an honor, a priviledge, a praise to serve the Almighty God. To be found worthy to serve him is a privildege as well as a pleasure. To serve the Lord gets easier and easier. It's just living right and wanting to do what's right. So if you really love the Lord. You will know it's an honor to be on the Lord side.

Salvation Belong To Everyone

You look at people and you may talk about them, because they are not saved. Quit saying if people would get saved and do what's right. Quit saying people just don't know how good it is to be saved. They ought to quit living like that. Quit saying people this and people that. Because remember you use to be one of those people. Who wasn't saved at once in your life. And you wasn't always were you are. Salvation belongs to all men. God is not willing any man should perish. But all men to come to repentance. So salvation belong to all and that's why God sent his son Jesus. So all will have a chance to get it right as you got it like that. Salvation belongs to all. And God made it like that.

57

We Are Saved By Grace

We are saved by grace. Nothing we have done. It's because of God goodness. He is not willing that any man should perish but all men comes to repentance. So tell those who are lost they can be saved. Because it's the grace of God. That keeps us saved.

58

Choose Heaven

At the end of this life where is your destination. Where will you end up. Where will you spend eternity. It's either Heaven or Hell. There is only two places you will go. The Bible says Luke 16:22 And it came to pass, that the beggar died, and was carried by the angels into Abraham's bosom: the rich man also died, and was buried. Luke16:23 And in hell he lift up his eyes, being in torments, and seeth Abraham afar off, and Lazarus in his bosom. You will go somewhere when you leave this world. Only you can choose where will you spend eternity. It's your choice.

You Want Leave This World Before Time

You want leave this world before time. When you leave this world it's because your time is up. Even as Jesus said no man taketh my life but he lay it down. John 10:18 No man taketh it from me, but I lay it down, of myself. I have power to lay it down, and I have power to take it again. This commandment have I received of my Father. Therefore you will only leave this world when God says your time is up not man.

Many Things Is Going To Change, But I Stay The Same

You see job titles change for some. Food appetites also change as well. You have summer, winter, spring, and fall. But I'm one person who never changes. I am Jesus Christ the Son of the most high God. I have power over life. I have power over death. So if you want to get close to me. You can find me in the Holy Bible. I'm one that never will change. I'm Alpha and Omega. The Beginning and the end. The First and The Last. I will never change. I will be here to the end.

61

Divine Destiny

Some things are just meant to happen and we can't change it. But one thing when you are serving God, he's got all the power in his hand. God knows what's planned for your life. He knows what you're going to do, before you do it. Whatever shape you're in. God knew you were going to be, in that shape you are in. But don't give up if the shape, you are in is bad. Keep going forward. For God knows what your divine destiny is. When your serving him, and it will turn out good.

62

Serving The Lord Will Pay Off

You may not know why, you keep having test after test. Trial after trial, But, if you read, God word he will tell you why. You will be tempted you will be tried. But, one thing you must remember, it will all pay off. You may not understand when. You may not understand how. But, you must know serving the Lord pays off. See, you must suffer when your saved. That's taking part of Jesus suffering. But it's good to suffer for Jesus name. It's good to suffer for serving God. But always remember, what you do for God. It will pay off.

Keep Your Eye On Jesus

Keep your eye on Jesus. You can never go wrong. If you keep your eye on Jesus. He will show you how to live life. He will fight for you. He will keep you from evil. If you are weak he will make you strong. So, if you keep your eye on Jesus. You will never go wrong. For keeping your eye on Jesus. He will strengthen you thru his word. And he will help you to stay strong. So keep your eye on Jesus. And you will never ever go wrong.

Staying Focus On God

Don't lose your focus, that's what the devil want you to do. Is to look the other way. But stay focus on God. That's why some people backslide. They be walking with God, and be on the right track obeying God. And, then they stop, praying reading God word and fasting, then they get caught up in the wrong things. Things that don't edify God. And they began to lose focus. Also the devil start sending tempts, distractions, their way so they can lose focus. Because the devil sees when you don't pray. He sees how you act when your not doing the things of God. So he tempt you, because your not doing the things of God. You fall for his tempts. So stay focus and keep your mind on Jesus. And you want fall when Satan comes to tempt you. Because you stayed focus.

65

Who Is God Using To Talk To You Thru

God may send someone to help you. So be careful how you treat people who come up to you. You may feel they are know one special. You may even feel they don't know what they are talking about. You just need to be careful when someone is saying something that's in the word. Because you don't know who, God is using to help you to get your break thru.

God Way Will Last

Any other way you live beside serving God want last. You want to live long on earth. Serve the Lord. You want peace. Serve the Lord. You want happiness. Serve the Lord. You want a successful future. Serve the Lord. You want a better way of living. Serve the the Lord for he is the way. And his way will last. But you have to give your life to him if you want to last. So serve the Lord, for God way will last.

Who Are You Serving God Are Man

God is the one who holds the whole world in his hand. Who do you have your trust in. Who do you have your confidence in. Man will fail you and that is true. You have to know who your putting your trust into. To see you thru. If you serve God and you will have life. He is the only one can help you out. Don't put your trust in man. Put your trust in God. For if man fail you. You will know God will help you out. Because you serve him there will always be a way out.

Come Unto Me

You keep following those things don't make a difference. Take a look at your life. Are you joyful or you proud who you are? Is there success or is it just getting by. If you follow me. I'll watch over you. I'll keep you from evil. Yes, troubles will come but I'll help you along the way. So come to me and I'll set you free. And you will see it's so easy to live life. If you will give your life to me.

69

Are You Powerful Or You Powerless

I send out power when you come in my presence. I send out power when you need it. You seem to forget how powerful I am when test come. You act like I'm not able to help you. You see when test comes it's to let you see what you need to work on. Because how you handle that test. Will let you see what's in you. I already know what you will do. So stay in my word, read daily, pray, fast often, not just when the preacher call one. You want power you got to do something. Because to whom do little will have little. It's not how long you have been saved. So are you powerful or you powerless.

Seek The Presence Of The Lord

In God presence is the fullness of joy. God will give you joy unspeakable and full of glory. If you would spend time with God. You will see God will give you everything you need. For in his presence is joy. In God presence things will turn around and work for your good. Stay in God presence and your joy will be restored.

Prayer Will Keep You

If you would pray. God will answer your prayer. He says seek me while I may be found. Call upon me while I am near. If you would just pray. God will keep you when you pray. Prayer can change any situation. And most of all prayer can keep you. If you would just pray.

You Got To Put God First

❈

You got to put God first and everything else will fall in place. God word says seek ye first the kingdom of God and all these things shall be added unto thee. God will add everything else when you seek him first. Everything else will come.

Things Will Get Better When You Trust God

When you trust God everything will work out. The Bible says to trust God with all your heart and lean not to your own understanding. When you trust God things will work out in your favour. For all thing worketh together for good for those who love God and to them who are the called according to his purpose. Romans 8:28

How Are You Living Now

The life you live will show God if you really want to serve him. The word of God says the tree is known by the fruit it bears. Whatever you are doing. And how you are living shows God if you want to serve him. It's not enough to come to Church on Sunday. And the rest of the week you don't live like you serve God. The things you do speaks for you. So how are you living.

You Can't Lose Serving God

You can't lose serving God. You will receive eternal life. See it's nothing wrong with leaving this world when you know you are going to be with the LORD. 2 Cor. 5:8 We are confident, I say, and willing rather to be absent from the body, and to be present with the LORD. So we can't lose serving God. Our reward is great.

Triles Don't Last Always

Trouble may come your way but they don't last always. You may be tried you may be tested. But remember, after the end of every test. You got the victory when you serve the Lord. Test will come and triles too. But remember who is in control of every test that try you. God is in control whatever you go thru. He want let the devil kill you. If you trust him to see you thru. So next time you are faced with a trile or a test. Say I know at the end of this test, I got the victory. For God is in control of this test.

Don't Back Up Go Forward

You're suppose to be forgetting those things behind you. And pressing toward those things before you. Why do you keep backing up instead of going forward. Remember what state you were in before, you got where you are? So why would you want to go backward, instead of forward? Remember Jesus is the one that set you free. So remember if ever you think about, you want to go backward. Remember the shape you were in before you got saved. That should make you want to go forward.

You Say You Got The Victory

You come to church sing the song. You got the victory. Do you really examine yourself? How do you act when faced with a test? How do you act when someone lie on you? How do you act when someone mistreat you? How do you act when people talk down to you? How do you act when your supervisor treat you wrong? If you got the victory you will do what my word say. You will bless them that curse you. You pray for them that despitefully use you. You want retaliate, but you will be kind anyway. And in doing so you will heap hot coals on their head. By doing that you will have the victory.

Don't Let The Devil Win

You may say things like. I don't like the devil. I'm not going to hell. I fear death etc. Well, what are you doing to deal with the devil. Are to keep from going to hell. Are how is your life style. You can't beat the devil without Jesus. If he tempted Jesus who are you. You must know it takes Jesus to fight for you.

80

God Can Refresh, Restore And Revive You

God can refresh you and give you back everything you may have lost. God can restore everything that may be dried up in your life. God can revive you and restore all the things you may feel may have dried up in your life. God is a restorer. He can give you back everything. He can give you double for all your trouble.

God Will Revive You

God sends his power to revive you. God knows just what you need and when you need it. He said I came that you might have life and that you may have it more abundantly. God will revive you and give you what you need.

Nothing Is Going To Happen Until You Speak To Your Situation

You have the power to speak to your situation. And it has to get in line. For God says life and death is in the power of the tongue. And you shall have whatsoever you say. Speak to your situation and God will back you up. Things have to get in line when you speak the word of God.

We Need Revival

When Revival comes. It comes to Revive you to wake up on the inside what may have been laying dormant. Revival comes to get you back on fire for God. You may have been through many trials and many test. But once you are revived. It gives you the strength to keep moving.

Jesus Has Already Won Your Victory

When Jesus went to Calvary he went for you and me. Now we can be forgiven of our sins. And without the shedding of the blood there is no remission. Jesus already won for you and me. So when you except Jesus Christ as your LORD and Saviour you will have the victory.

85

Your Time Has Already Come

You are now living in your now. Your time has come. The wait is over. Now walk into the destiny God has planned for you from the foundation of the earth. Even as God told Jeremiah before I formed you in the belly I knew thee: It's Now. Your Time Is Now. Jeremiah 1:5 Before I formed thee in the belly I knew thee; and before thou camest forth out of the womb I sanctified thee, and I ordained thee a prophet unto the nations. Your Time Has Arrived.

You Are On The Winning Team

When you serve God you are on the winning team. God have great plans for our life. And to give us an expected end. To be on the LORD side is awesome. Because when troubles comes nothing can't overcome you when you serve God. For he will fight your battles for you. 2 Chron. 20:15 for the battle is not yours, but God's.

Victory Is Yours

In the name of Jesus we have the victory. Jesus already won every battle we must go through. The fight already been fixed from the beginning. For God is Alpha and Omega. He is the beginning and the end. And he have everything under control. He already knows how your end will turn out. Because your steps has already been order by him. Psalm 37:23 The steps of a good man are ordered by the LORD: and he delighteth in his way.

You Keep On Going The Other Way

You go around telling people you are saved, But you keep on going the other way. You quote my word and know it. But you keep on going the other way. You even pray, fast, and confess my word. But you keep on going the other way. You see I see everything you say and you do. You get in church shout, cry pray in tongues, jerk like you feel something. But you keep on going the other way. You better quit playing with me. Don't you know I'm real, you don't have to pretend. You need to remember there is a judgement at the end. Thank You Lord.

89

Quit Deceiving Yourself

~ ❋ ~

You go around saying I'm saved. But, yet you can say I'm going out. You can walk around drinking you can sing the blues, no different in how the world is doing. But, yet you say your saved. If your saved why are you still doing the same things you was doing before you got saved. Old things should be passed away. And behold all things you do should be new. How come there's no change. Quit deceiving yourself. You are not saved.

Consider Your Ways

Have you took a look at how you're living? Have you took a look at the kind of conversation you hold? Have you took a look at the places you're going? Have you considered what you're doing? Is what you're doing lining up with what God word says, you suppose to be doing. If not consider your ways. And ask God to save you and to make you into being what he want you to be. Consider your ways. So you will be ready when it's judgment day.

Don't Look To The Left

Don't go thru life looking one way. Just because the way you did it may not have turned out right. But, have you tried Jesus to let him be your guide. If you get saved and let Jesus become your savior. Then you want have to look to the left. You will always look to the right. For it will be Jesus who will be guiding your life. And you will never go wrong again for the rest of your life. As long as you allow Jesus to guide your life.

You Keep On Messing Up

You keep on messing up time and time again. What's it going to take for you to get it right within. You don't have to keep messing up. I'm able to pick you up. To keep you from messing up. You just need to make up your mind. That you are going to let me help you. So that you can quit messing up.

93

How Come You Keep Being Defeated

You keep on being defeated. The devil laughs, when he see he keep's winning in your life. Don't you know you can't defeat the devil in your own power. I'm the one who have the power Jesus Christ the son of God. So let me fight for you and then and then only. Can you quit being defeated. For I will win the battle that keep's defeating you.

What's It Going To Take For You To Get It Right

───※───

You keep doing the same thing. Keep going the same places. Year after year. Month after month, day after day, hour after hour. Still you are in the same shape you were in years ago. You should be tired of being defeated. You have tried your way and there's still know change. If you try God way. He will never fail you. He will show you a better way to live. If you try him you will see your life will be fulfill. But only if you will except Jesus Christ as your Lord and savior he will come in.

Quit Doing Things Because It Feels Good

You may see a fruit and it looks good. And you eat it because it looks good. But you had instructions from your doctor not to eat it, because it's not good for you. Everything looks good is not good for you. And because it feel right, don't make it right for you to do. Even in God word he has statuses, commandments that we must follow. We can't do what we want to do. Because we want too. We have to do what God word tells us to do. We have keep God commandments. If we want to stay right with God. We can't do what we want to do. If what we want to do. Is not what is right.

Don't Ge t Un focus

All the power I'm sending out you keep going left. You go right for a while, but you go left again. You got to stay focus on me. You can't afford to get weary in well doing. The devil never get tired. That's why you got to keep on your amour at all times. So you will be able to stand against the wiles of the devil. Never get slothful in serving me. Stay in the word and you will be excited. And full of joy at all times. Don't loose focus for the devil will always be around unto Jesus comes back. So stay focus on the Lord and you want ever get slack.

If It Don't Edify God It Will End

If what your doing is not edifying God it will end. You may keep doing wrong. But one day you will see your not accomplishing anything for all the wrong you been doing. You keep getting it wrong. year after year, month after month. And still your not living right. You should be tired of the life you are living. You keep feeling depressed, tired, rundown, looking rougher, and rougher, still you are not living any better. Can't you see the way your living it's not edifying God, That's why you keep struggling everyday of your life. Get it right with God and you will have a better life. When you surrender your life to God. Then God can help you to have a second chance at life, to get it right. Give your life to God get it right. Before it's to late. And you don't have a second chance at life.

Doing Wrong Will Come Back On You

When a person do wrong to someone. That is not the end of it. God sees and he knows all. God wants you to treat your neighbor right. God want you to do right by your neighbor. For Jesus say by this you will know my disciples. For they have love one for another. If someone is treating you wrong. You know it's not God. For God is a God of love.

What You Do Today May Come Back On You One Day

Sometimes I believe some people really think they will get away with how they mistreat someone. That is why you don't commit adultery with someone else husband or wife. Because if you ever get married someone will mess with your wife or husband. And what can you say. Now I am reaping what I sowed because I did it to someone. Now you know how that person feels that's why you don't do that. The Bible says let every man have his own wife. And the same goes to every woman have your own husband.

How Can You Mess With Someone Life. But You Want Things To Go Right For You

I look at how someone may treat someone wrong. And they really think it's okay. But not with God. He sees and he knows. And he will give every man according to what he does. How can you want your life to be happy. But you are messing with someone else life. Just remember everything you give out will come back to you. It's just a matter of time.

I would like to thank God for he has given me many books to write. This was my second book that I wrote many years ago. But just recently God has given me many other Books to write about. Which I have other books that has been publish and are available. But I publish each one as God lets me know that it is time for the ones he want me to bring forward. They all have an appointed time that God has for me to bring them forward for his glory. I thank God for choosing me to write this book. He could have chosen anyone but he chose me. Thank you Jesus for choosing me.

I am really proud of the God I serve. He give wisdom to anyone that serve him. And, I know it was God that gave me the wisdom and knowledge to be a writer for him.

This book was written in 11 days. I know for certain this was God. I thank God the Father, Jesus his Son, and Precious Holy Spirit. For choosing me to be a messenger for him. God he is the one who gets all the glory for every book I write. God giveth and I write it. God gets all the glory. I love the God Head. I have written several books and I publish them as the Lord would have me to. In his timing.

Thank You
Jesus

God the Father
Jesus his Son
And precious
Holy Spirit
By: Bren Daniels
Jesus The Writer

Notes

Notes

BE BLESSED

Printed in the United States
By Bookmasters